QuoteOctopus.com

The best quotes

Publisher Contact

257 Swanston Street, Melbourne, VIC, AUSTRALIA

Email: hello@quoteoctopus.com

Social media: facebook.com/quoteoctopus

Acknowledgements

The team at Quote Octopus would like to thank our friends, family, suppliers and customers for making our vision of creating the highest-quality books a reality. Thanks for purchasing and enjoy the quotes!

This page is intentionally left blank

This page is intentionally left blank

A criminal trial is never about seeking justice for the victim. If it were, there could be only one verdict: guilty.

Alan Dershowitz

A good lawyer knows how to shut up when he's won his case.

Alan Dershowitz

A visit to Israel is always an experience in cognitive dissonance. The Israel you personally see and hear is so completely different from the Israel you read and hear about in the media.

Alan Dershowitz

All sides in a trial want to hide at least some of the truth.

Alan Dershowitz

Any human being has private thoughts.

Alan Dershowitz

Asymmetrical warfare is a euphemism for terrorism, just like collateral damage is a euphemism for killing innocent civilians.

Alan Dershowitz

Being offended by freedom of speech should never be regarded as a justification for violence.

Alan Dershowitz

Candor and accountability in a democracy is very important. Hypocrisy has no place.

Alan Dershowitz

Doing something because God has said to do it does not make a person moral: it merely tells us that person is a prudential believer, akin to the person who obeys the command of an all-powerful secular king.

Alan Dershowitz

Ed Koch will never 'rest in peace.' That was not his way. He was always nervously squirming, while making others squirm as well. Comfort was not his goal. He understood that to be a proud and assertive Jew meant never being able to leave a sigh of relief and say, 'It's over, we are at peace, we can now put down our guard and relax.'

Alan Dershowitz

Every celebrity case I've been involved in - I've been involved in a great many - the one thing you can be sure of is they don't get the same justice as everybody else. It could be worse, it could be better, it's never the same.

Alan Dershowitz

Every lawsuit results from somebody doing something wrong. If everybody did right, we wouldn't need laws.

Alan Dershowitz

For most people, the question why be good - as distinguished from merely law abiding - is a simple one. Because God commands it, because the Bible requires it, because good people go to Heaven and bad people go to Hell.

Alan Dershowitz

Freedom of speech means freedom for those who you despise, and freedom to express the most despicable views. It also means that the government cannot pick and choose which expressions to authorize and which to prevent.

Alan Dershowitz

Good character consists of recognizing the selfishness that inheres in each of us and trying to balance it against the altruism to which we should all aspire. It is a difficult balance to strike, but no definition of goodness can be complete without it.

Alan Dershowitz

Great research universities must insist on independence from government and on the exercise of academic freedom.

Alan Dershowitz

Hypocrisy is not a way of getting back to the moral high ground. Pretending you're moral, saying your moral is not the same as acting morally.

Alan Dershowitz

I am a peace supporting Jew.

Alan Dershowitz

I am deeply concerned that, without peace and a two-state solution, the Jewish and democratic nature of Israel is in danger. That's why I have opposed Israel's settlement policy since 1973, and that's why I have favored a two-state solution since 1967.

Alan Dershowitz

I believe that if Israel were to put an end to the settlements in the West Bank tomorrow, as it did in Gaza, there would still be reluctance on the part of the Palestinian Authority to recognize Israel's right to exist as a Jewish secular democracy.

Alan Dershowitz

I came from a poor family, so working and going to school at the same time was natural. It taught me multi-tasking, although we didn't call it that back then. I learned I could never be idle, I need to be doing many things at once.

Alan Dershowitz

I can't find anything in the Constitution that says you prefer the life of the mother, or the convenience of the mother if it's an abortion by choice, over the potential life of the fetus. Look, I think women, if they're required to not have abortions, could die and could - so I favor a woman's right to choose.

Alan Dershowitz

I charge my wealthy clients a lot and put 10 per cent in a fund which I use to pay the expenses of my poorer clients. When the government gangs up on the poor schnook in the street, someone has to stand up for him.

Alan Dershowitz

I don't believe in firing professors. They have academic freedom.

Alan Dershowitz

I don't think the law exists to arrive at the truth. If it did, we wouldn't have exclusionary rules, we wouldn't have presumptions of innocence, we wouldn't have proof beyond reasonable doubt. There's an enormous difference between the role of truth in law and the role of truth in science. In law, truth is one among many goals.

Alan Dershowitz

I feel like my 50 years at Harvard were an interlude. I'm really a New Yorker.

Alan Dershowitz

I generally don't select my chicken or my hamburgers based on the personal ideology of the person who is either flipping the hamburgers or making the money back at corporate headquarters. But if people want to do that, they're free to do it.

Alan Dershowitz

I have been defending Israel's right to exist, and to defend itself against terrorism, for many years-on college campuses, in television appearances and in debate.

Alan Dershowitz

I know Obama, I like Obama, I voted for Obama.

Alan Dershowitz

I love discomfort. I mean, my whole life is discomfort. One reason I can never retire is that the idea of just sitting on the beach totally comfortable is not a desideratum in my life. I like ambiguity, I like conflict, I like uncertainly.

Alan Dershowitz

I love the Bible.

Alan Dershowitz

I love to play. I love, opera, hiking and museums. The one thing I don't do is sit. I have a tremendous amount of energy.

Alan Dershowitz

I never do anything for money; I get paid a lot of money as a by-product.

Alan Dershowitz

I never had a strategy about my life. I didn't have enough information to have a strategy. I'm the first person in my family to go to college. I had no family mentors.

Alan Dershowitz

I never had an existential moment when I asked myself what I was going to do. I always wanted to be a lawyer, and I knew exactly the kind of lawyer I wanted to be.

Alan Dershowitz

I never place limits on the potential success of my students. If they're going into acting, they're going to win the Oscar... If they're going into law, they're going to be chief justice.

Alan Dershowitz

I talk with my hands. Some people don't like that. That's who I am.

Alan Dershowitz

I tell my students, if you ever become comfortable with your role as criminal defense lawyer, it's time to quit. It should be a constant source of discomfort, because you're dealing with incredible moral ambiguity, and you've been cast into a role which is not enviable.

Alan Dershowitz

I think extremists within the base may very well move the Democratic party away from its pro-Israel position.

Alan Dershowitz

I think mistakes are the essence of science and law. It's impossible to conceive of either scientific progress or legal progress without understanding the important role of being wrong and of mistakes.

Alan Dershowitz

I think most defense attorneys honestly believe the principle that says, 'Better 10 guilty go free than even one possibly innocent person be convicted.'

Alan Dershowitz

I think that lawyers are terrible at admitting that they're wrong. And not just admitting it - also realizing it.

Alan Dershowitz

I think that lawyers are terrible at admitting that they're wrong. And not just admitting it; also realizing it. Most lawyers are very successful, and they think that because they're making money and people think well of them, they must be doing everything right.

Alan Dershowitz

I think there would be less torture with a warrant requirement than without one.

Alan Dershowitz

I think we're seeing privacy diminish, not by laws... but by young people who don't seem to value their privacy.

Alan Dershowitz

I understand that it's good tactics to categorize me as a close-minded, unobjective extremist, but nobody that respects me has those views.

Alan Dershowitz

I was a Jewish rabbinical student for 12 years, and studied the Bible all the time.

Alan Dershowitz

I was critical of race-based affirmative action early on in my career and I've changed my mind. And I've publicly acknowledged that I was wrong.

Alan Dershowitz

I'm a very tough guy, and I fight hard, and I don't give up. And that makes me friends and that makes me enemies, and I know that.

Alan Dershowitz

I'm never satisfied unless I get the last word.

Alan Dershowitz

I'm not a single-issue person, but I spend so much time on Israel because it is so unfairly condemned around the world.

Alan Dershowitz

I'm worried about privacy because of the young people who don't give a damn about their privacy, who are prepared to put their entire private lives online. They put stuff on Facebook that 15 years from now will prevent them from getting the jobs they want. They don't understand that they are mortgaging their future for a quick laugh from a friend.

Alan Dershowitz

I've had such a satisfying life professionally and personally. I hope my tombstone says, 'Never boring.'

Alan Dershowitz

I've thought hard about my psychological connections and I think I've managed to separate out the psychological from the legal, moral, and political.

Alan Dershowitz

I've thought of publishing a book of my hate mail, but I don't own the rights to the letters.

Alan Dershowitz

I've written important articles on prevention, on the concept of the preventive state, how the law is moving much more in an area of trying to prevent wrongs than trying to deal with them after they occur. That will be my academic/intellectual legacy.

Alan Dershowitz

Ideas don't desert you; ideas aren't treasonous to you, but people can be.

Alan Dershowitz

If America has the right to target Osama bin Laden, or terrorists, of course Israel has the right to defend itself from terrorism.

Alan Dershowitz

If torture is going to be administered as a last resort in the ticking-bomb case, to save enormous numbers of lives, it ought to be done openly, with accountability, with approval by the president of the United States or by a Supreme Court justice.

Alan Dershowitz

If you're a prosecutor, and you believe the defendant is guilty, you only talk about ultimate truth, but not intermediate truth. If you're the defense attorney, you care deeply about intermediate truth, but you tend to neglect ultimate truth.

Alan Dershowitz

In my neighborhood, everyone had an opinion on the local cantor. You didn't go to a synagogue to listen to the rabbi's sermon. You went to listen to the cantor. It was like a concert.

Alan Dershowitz

In some ways, Israel has achieved a peace. There are fewer rockets being sent into Sderot, there are no rockets to speak of from the North, there has been very little terrorism from the West Bank. It's a kind of peace. I hope for a better and more enduring peace. Peace is not an endgame; we will never be completely at peace.

Alan Dershowitz

In the Pentagon Papers case, the government asserted in the Supreme Court that the publication of the material was a threat to national security. It turned out it was not a threat to U.S. security. But even if it had been, that doesn't mean that it couldn't be published.

Alan Dershowitz

In the real world in which we live, you always have to choose between evils. And in choosing between evils, you have to have moral criteria for how to make those choices.

Alan Dershowitz

In today's distorted world of 'human rights,' truth takes a back seat to ideology, and false claims - especially those that 'support' radical ideologies - persist even after they have been exposed.

Alan Dershowitz

Individuals have the right to pick and choose which expressions to condemn, which to praise and which to say nothing about. Governments, however, must remain neutral as to the content of expression. And governments must protect the rights of all to express even the most despicable of views.

Alan Dershowitz

Israel can't make peace without the clear support of the United States.

Alan Dershowitz

It simply cannot be disputed that for decades the Palestinian leadership was more interested in there not being a Jewish state than in there being a Palestinian state.

Alan Dershowitz

It's every lawyer's dream to help shape the law, not just react to it.

Alan Dershowitz

It's much better to have rules that we can actually live within. And absolute prohibitions, generally, are not the kind of rules that countries would live within.

Alan Dershowitz

It's never acceptable to target civilians. It violates the Geneva Accords, it violates the international law of war and it violates all principles of morality.

Alan Dershowitz

It's wrong, and it's racist, and it's bigoted to say that guns are quintessentially American.

Alan Dershowitz

Judges are the weakest link in our system of justice, and they are also the most protected.

Alan Dershowitz

Juries are not computers. They are composed of human beings who evaluate evidence differently.

Alan Dershowitz

Laws are important precisely because in a democracy they reflect the attitudes and aspirations of those they govern.

Alan Dershowitz

Most liberal democracies don't try to figure out what the truth is.

Alan Dershowitz

My goal is always to keep support for Israel a bi-partisan issue and never make a national election any kind of referendum on Israel.

Alan Dershowitz

No country in the history of the world has ever contributed more to humankind and accomplished more for its people in so brief a period of time as Israel has done since its relatively recent rebirth in 1948.

Alan Dershowitz

On television and in the movies, crimes are always solved. Nothing is left uncertain. By the end, the viewer knows whodunit. In real life, on the other hand, many murders remain unsolved, and even some that are 'solved' to the satisfaction of the police and prosecutors lack sufficient evidence to result in a conviction.

Alan Dershowitz

President Obama has earned my vote on the basis of his excellent judicial appointments, his consensus-building foreign policy and the improvements he has brought about in the disastrous economy he inherited.

Alan Dershowitz

Real heroes are those who face death for a principle - say, to save the lives of others - without any promise of reward.

Alan Dershowitz

Scientists search for truth. Philosophers search for morality. A criminal trial searches for only one result: proof beyond a reasonable doubt.

Alan Dershowitz

The Internet knows no national borders.

Alan Dershowitz

The Israeli military plays more than a critical role in defending the citizens of the Jewish state. It also plays an important social, scientific and psychological role in preparing its young citizens for the challenging task of being Israelis in a difficult world.

Alan Dershowitz

The court of last resort is no longer the Supreme Court. It's 'Nightline.'

Alan Dershowitz

The defendant wants to hide the truth because he's generally guilty. The defense attorney's job is to make sure the jury does not arrive at that truth.

Alan Dershowitz

The law is agnostic about truth. It's very skeptical of ultimate truth. That's why freedom of speech permits lies to be told.

Alan Dershowitz

The law is agnostic about truth.

Alan Dershowitz

The pervasiveness of guns in our society is destroying America.

Alan Dershowitz

The prosecution wants to make sure the process by which the evidence was obtained is not truthfully presented, because, as often as not, that process will raise questions.

Alan Dershowitz

The sad reality is that there are no purely domestic issues in Israel. Issues that would be dealt with by municipalities in other countries - such as how to deal with a dangerous bridge or how to resolve conflicts between religious and secular bus riders - become major international issues when they occur in Israel.

Alan Dershowitz

The same independence that got me into trouble in high school got me praise in college.

Alan Dershowitz

The struggle for morality never stays won. It's always in process.

Alan Dershowitz

The threat or fear of violence should not become an excuse or justification for restricting freedom of speech.

Alan Dershowitz

The vast majority of gun owners don't kill, but people who do kill, tend to kill with guns, and often with illegal guns.

Alan Dershowitz

The very concept of an Iranian university is an oxymoron. There are no free and open places of learning in that repressive theocracy. Dissenters are not given tenure; they are murdered, after first being tortured. Blasphemy, which is broadly defined, is punished. Gays are not only excluded from Iranian universities, but are imprisoned and killed.

Alan Dershowitz

The worst mistake you can make is underrating your enemy. Assuming that they're evil - I think it's a terrible thing to do.

Alan Dershowitz

There are many levels of truth.

Alan Dershowitz

There are two kinds of terrorism. Rational terrorism such as Palestinian terrorism and apocalyptic terrorism like Sept. 11. You have to distinguish between the two.

Alan Dershowitz

There is a paranoid streak in American life. Radio talk show hosts tend to foment that paranoid streak in American life.

Alan Dershowitz

There will never be another Ed Koch. He was an original, but he represented a significant, if shrinking, segment of American Jewry who refused to compromise their liberal values, their support for Israel or their Jewish pride.

Alan Dershowitz

There's no evidence that I'm aware of that guns protect liberty.

Alan Dershowitz

There's no evidence that I'm aware of that guns reduce crime.

Alan Dershowitz

Twenty five percent of Israeli citizens are not even Jewish. Anybody can become an Israeli citizen if you qualify. Religion is not a criterion for citizenship.

Alan Dershowitz

We all learn in school that the judicial, legislative and executive branches of government must check and balance each other. But other non state institutions must participate in this important system of checks and balances as well. These checking institutions include the academy, the media, religious institutions and NGOs.

Alan Dershowitz

We don't have an Official Secrets Act in the United States, as other countries do. Under the First Amendment, freedom of the press, freedom of speech, and freedom of association are more important than protecting secrets.

Alan Dershowitz

We have to fulfill what the real meaning of the Second Amendment is: reasonable access to guns for self-protection and for hunting. And there's no room in America for these semiautomatic, automatic and other kinds of weapons that are simply designed to cause mass havoc.

Alan Dershowitz

Well you know, all law is about injustice.

Alan Dershowitz

Well, first of all, no professor should be able to say, I refuse to defend my position. I refuse to debate my position.

Alan Dershowitz

Well, many insane people and seriously mentally ill people seem very reasonable.

Alan Dershowitz

What the United States has to do is send a clear message to Iran that they will not be able to develop nuclear weapons. Why endure the difficulty of sanctions if they are not going to be able to develop nuclear weapons anyway?

Alan Dershowitz

When I decide who to vote for as president, I ask myself who will be best for America and for the world. An important component of my answer involves my assessment of the candidate's willingness and ability to protect Israel's security, since I strongly believe that a strong Israel serves the interests of the United States and of world peace.

Alan Dershowitz

When I was 14 or 15, a camp counselor told me I was smart. I had never been very good in school, but he told me once that I was smart but my mind operated a little differently.

Alan Dershowitz

When I was growing up, my mother would always say, 'It will go on your permanent record.' There was no 'permanent record.' If there were a 'permanent record,' I'd never be able to be a lawyer. I was such a bum in elementary school and high school... There is a permanent record today, and it's called the Internet.

Alan Dershowitz

When you discriminate against anyone, you discriminate against everyone. It's a display of terrible intolerance.

Alan Dershowitz

You can't think about terrorism without thinking about Palestinian terrorism. Palestinians began international terrorism. It started with them in 1968. They used it as the first resort, not the last resort. They invented it, they perfected it, they benefited from it and they taught the world how to use it and that it would be successful.

Alan Dershowitz

You know, it's ironic to me that Christians want to keep the Ten Commandments in our schools, because Christianity has abrogated four of the Ten Commandments. For example, the Sabbath day according to the Ten Commandments is Saturday, not Sunday. And the reason is because God rested, not because Jesus was resurrected.

Alan Dershowitz

You're absolutely right: Bob Grant is a racist, Bob Grant is a bigot, he's a despicable talk show host and I agree with that.

Alan Dershowitz

This page is intentionally left blank

This page is intentionally left blank

This page is intentionally left blank

This page is intentionally left blank

This page is intentionally left blank

www.ingramcontent.com/pod-product-compliance
Lightning Source LLC
Chambersburg PA
CBHW061932280526
45787CB00004B/1583